THOUGHTS ON BEING A MOMMY

By

Karla Borglum Santoro

Illustrated by
Tracy Lynn Doty

Windswept Press
Interlaken, NY
1992

Manufactured in the United States of America

A *quality* publication by
Windswept Press
Interlaken, New York 14847

Thoughts on
Being a Mommy

DEDICATION

This book is dedicated to my husband, Mark, my son, Justin, and my daughter, Rachel, for without them there would be no *Thoughts* . . .

ACKNOWLEDGMENTS

And Special Thanks To:

Suzanne B. Coleates for polishing my dream and for all her encouragement.

Tracy Lynn Doty for persevering with a new twist of her pen.

All the women who took the time to read the manuscript and give me their opinion on the pages.

My mom, Norma J. Borglum, for being my best friend.

THOUGHTS ON BEING A MOMMY

From the author . . .

Ever since I can remember, I have been writing. Journals were kept from about the eighth grade and continued on and off until just recently, when I found a journal, two baby books, books for children, and this book too much to keep up with.

The decision to keep detailed and up-to-date baby books came after viewing my own baby book and being disappointed at the blank pages. Now that I am a mom I want to know everything about my infancy and childhood. Unfortunately, writing did not come so compulsively to my Mother so I have to be content with what she can recollect.

My journal topics took a very limited subject range after children entered our household. Topics used to consist of husband, job and dog; now they are mere footnotes to kids, kids, kids. After experimenting with different styles of recording thoughts on life with children and on my new title of mom, I discovered the delight in addressing some areas of joy and concern to other mothers. In sharing my thoughts with friends, I found a common ground. I realized early on the best way to get the most out of my mothering role was to talk to other moms. The darkest moments are reduced to giggles when another mom shares a similar moment. The realization of not being alone in this has brought indescribable relief.

So, the purpose of this book comes in two parts: first, to record my thoughts for my children to read after they become parents and have all the questions I have had (please note entries are by no means in chronological order); second, to help at least one mom feel less lonely in the most important, most rewarding, most difficult job she'll ever undertake.

THOUGHTS ON BEING A MOMMY

Some days I am the best mom in the whole world. My children are stimulated intellectually with projects requiring fine motor skill action. The results are displayed to boost self esteem. We make messes and it does not bother me in the least. The children spend several hours outdoors developing their large motor skills and exercising. We read books, make books, and act out stories. Lunch includes fresh cut up vegetables and whole grains. My voice never rises above polite decibels. We laugh a lot.

Some days I more closely resemble the Wicked Witch of the West or an army drill sergeant.

Sometimes single and/or childless friends want to know something about what it is like to be a parent. The best I can come up with is: after a child enters your home, your physical and mental feelings are heightened to degrees you never imagined possible. One has never before experienced such exhaustion, impatience, frustration, or fright. However, one has also never experienced such happiness, pride or love.

Rachel usually takes a nap during church. Once she is asleep so even the liveliest hymn does not cause her eyelids to flutter, I still supply her with that rocking motion. "Why do I keep rocking?" I asked myself. I realized that for a few precious moments I am oblivious to everyone, devoting to her my utmost attention, my whole being. Often at home I feel too busy to hold her while she is napping. Before my eyes—in a blink— she will no longer need, or want, to sleep in my arms. I want to rock her every moment I can get in, now, while I don't have to share being the most important person in her life.

Some of the best talks with my son happen during ice cream snacks—either dripping from a stick on the back steps in the sun, or in bowls at the kitchen table. Usually I ask him what he would like to talk about. We have discussed in various degrees of depth, family trips to the moon, anger, sadness, God, heaven, ABC's, Daddy, Rachel, when Justin was a baby, being gentle to pets, opposites, rhyming words, cooking . . . I treasure these talks. I have developed a new fondness for ice cream.

It is the law of motherhood that as soon as it is Daddy's turn to get up with the kids they sleep until 7:00 a.m., when for you they greet the morning at 6:00 a.m.

War, violence take on a whole new horrendous meaning when you are a mother. At one time all those soldiers, fighting and dying, were three year olds playing with clothespins on a shoebox, just like mine is doing now.

Sometimes it is a beautiful, warm world to introduce to my children. Sometimes it is rainbows and flowers, plush gardens, music, love, hugs and kisses, friends, smiles and laughter, a full cookie jar.

Sometimes it is a dangerous, scary world. Sometimes all I can think about is someone hurting or taking them. I think about the chemicals they breathe, the garbage they see, a war that may happen in their lifetime. Sometimes it is dark clouds, hate, violence, strangers, frowns and cries, hunger.

Usually it is a healthy, necessary mixture of the two, with more thought and time given to the first description, more prayer given to the second.

Our pediatrician thinks I don't listen to him concerning facts on fevers. He explains fevers are the body's way of fighting infection, fevers are good, fevers are generally nothing to worry about. But Justin's was 103 degrees even after fever-reducing medication and a few days of antibiotics to treat a bad ear infection. Concerned, I called the doctor's office and a stronger antibiotic was prescribed. Still Justin's temperature was 103–1/2 degrees last night and again this morning. An appointment was made. The key, the doctor explains, is Justin's behavior when his temperature is normal. So, okay, I admit it is close to his everyday action. But, I want to explain how he appears when his fever is high: his beautiful, sparkling eyes are red and glazed; his usual active, inquisitive self is lying indifferent on the couch or asking to go up for a nap. "See you tomorrow," he said to me as I tucked him in at 4:00 pm. It is scary to me.

And there is the story I heard about a little girl—a toddler daughter of a friend of a friend. Her parents tucked her in for the night after giving her medication for a fever. When they checked on her a few hours later, they found her lifeless. Those are the facts I remember every time my children have a fever. Maybe I should get more facts, but I know there are no definite answers.

My logical, common sense part tells me not to worry so, to give the antibiotics another day before calling the doctor's office. This wise part of me can see and understand the normal symptoms of physical illness. But sometimes when my children, my babies, are sick and so unlike themselves, my irrational love for them overrides my wiser self, and I need to have their doctor say they will be fine. Sometimes my imagination needs settling. The time and money involved are of no concern to me.

So, doctors, please continue being patient with me and other moms like me. We hear the facts you attempt to transfer, but cannot always apply them. We are crazy in love with our little people as you are with yours, but we need the comfort of your knowledge to support us through these sometimes frightening circumstances. Our children are irreplaceable, and we can't afford to take any chances.

Sometimes I can dig up patience where I thought there was none, be consistent one more time than I thought I could be, ask for something politely when all I want to do is yell and demand, smile when those muscles seem all used up . . . sometimes I can be a better mom for one more minute if I imagine someone is watching. The person reminds me to do my best because of the young, impressionable minds at stake being nurtured and guided by my actions and reactions. Sometimes I imagine it is a friend watching, listening at the door. Sometimes it is my husband, home from work early, listening to his family. But most of the time it is God; however, with Him I am not imagining His watching.

Reading books with my kids is one of my absolute favorite things to do. Being a teacher was a good excuse to read, collect, and buy children's books. But now that I am a mom I can explain confidently to my husband the purchase of yet another book is enriching their lives, boosting their creativity, encouraging them to continue being interested in the art form of reading. While I certainly believe this to be true, I have to admit I get a rush—an inner core feeling of true excitement—when I add another book to our ever increasing library. I even experience an instant high from the smell of a library. Sometimes I fantasize about being snowed in at the local bookroom, stuck with nothing to do all day but read books and smell the air. What can I say, books are my dear friends.

Now that I am a parent I can relive favorite children's tales and dive into all the more recent editions. Sometimes I forget my children are beside me as I become angry when Cinderella's nasty step-sisters tear her beautiful gown and I get goose bumps when the glass slipper fits her tiny foot. *Amy, The Dancing Bear*, by Carly Simon, with its beautifully flowing verse, is a sure cure for insomniacs, big and small. *The Birthday Moon*, by Lois Duncan lets my imagination run free. The old standby, *Make Way For Ducklings*, by Robert McCloskey, leaves me with a warm feeling of contentment. *Love You, Forever*, by Robert Munsch, puts a tear in your eye and a lump in your throat (be sure to read it alone before attempting to read it to your kids). I could go on and on.

Sometimes, in our everyday business, we have a

chance to act out a story we know. After numerous readings of *The Growing Up Feet*, by Beverely Cleary, we happened to be in need of a pair of puddle boots ourselves. Justin, then two, and I visited a nearby shoe store where we found red puddle boots just like Jimmy and Janet's! The young salesman was a bit perplexed when we asked him if his name was Mr. Markle, like in our story, but he was smiling when we left. So were we.

Blueberries For Sal, by Robert McCloskey, was never a story I imagined we would have a chance to bring to life. But as luck would have it, a girlfriend clued me in on a new and wonderful blueberry farm nearby—The Sugar Shack it is called. Justin and I planned to go, reviewing our book first, our only source of information on blueberries. We were not disappointed. The Sugar Shack people took us by tractor and wagon over a hill, leading us to bushes loaded with plump blueberries. They even supplied pails. Justin and I listened many times for a "kuplink, kuplank, kuplunk" as we dropped berries in our buckets. He kept asking, "Are we on Blueberry Hill?" We will never forget that day because the berries are in the freezer to remind us. Although, I have yet to get him to taste a blueberry.

Once he and I cut an orange felt triangle patch to cover a hole in a pair of his sweatpants. We decided to leave everything on a table overnight to see if the elves would come and sew it like they did for the shoemaker. Sure enough, they did. Recently when those pants were put in the rag pile, I felt a little sad. Maybe the elves will have to visit again.

My obvious enthusiasm is contagious. Even Rachel, at eight months, exhibits delight when she realizes I'm gathering books for us to read. When she holds a sturdy paged book and turns the pages while babbling, Justin will exclaim, "Look, Mom, she's reading!" My children approach me at various times and places, book in hand, requesting a story. They know there is a very good chance I will drop whatever it is I am doing to take a book break. It's just another plus side to being a mommy.

Love is reading their favorite books every night at least five times, for at least fourteen days in a row, or until their favorite title changes.

I am so proud of my boy and his manners. He uses "please," "thank you," and "you're welcome" at nearly every appropriate moment (this month, anyway). Why, just the other day he thanked me for having a potty for him. And just this morning while we were hanging clothes on the line together, I showed him that the chocolate came out of his blue shirt. "Why, thank you, Mommy." I promised to teach him how to get chocolate out of shirts when he gets bigger. I like polite manners—they are a wholesome sign of respect—they make me feel good.

My husband is often doing something Justin would like to try. We promise he can do it when he is older, which he interprets as: when he is a "man." He knows he can shave, use a drill, and attend meetings when he becomes a man. He decided, too, that he will be able to drink out of a glass glass when he is a man. So . . . just the other day we were watching a male gymnast perform floor exercises. I commented on how I wish I could do that. My boy assured me, "When you are a man you can, mom. When you are a man."

Love is putting a beautiful snail shell, with snail living inside, in your pocket to give your snail-shell-loving child, when you are certain the little critter will stick its slick, wet head out the next time you reach in.

Today Rachel was the most beautiful I have ever seen her. All kids have days where they are especially photogenic—today was one for her. I could not take my eyes off her. I marveled that such an exquisite being could be a part of me. This happens often with my son, too. Many pictures have been taken on his especially handsome days. I feel my children are the most beautiful, and while I'm at it, the most intelligent of their kind. It's a real compliment to another child if I think to myself, "He/she is almost as cute as Justin/Rachel."

Once I somewhat kiddingly said to my mom that my girlfriends with little girls must realize how beautiful my daughter is in comparison to their own (rather bold of me don't you think?). My mom informed me that all mothers think their child or children are the most beautiful, the most special. I thought about that. How wonderful it would be for each child born to have a mother, or someone, who believed him to be the best. What an impact it would have on society . . . on the world . . . if every child had that feeling, that knowledge—under his belt, tucked deep in his pocket—engraved in his heart: There is someone who thinks I am beautiful, who thinks I am special, who thinks I am the best.

Everytime I look in on my daughter so peacefully sleeping in her crib, surrounded by plush animals, covered with soft hand-made, quilted or satin-edged blankets, I wish, for a moment, to feel a sense of what it must be like to be two years of age.

Can you imagine what it would be like to have someone clean up your every spill? To take a nap as long as you liked? To sleep as late as you wished in the morning? To have every meal prepared for you and served on a teddy-bear stenciled, three-sectioned plate? To have some-one help you get dressed, comb your hair, brush your teeth, trim your nails? To spend your day playing with toys? To cuddle up next to a big person and have your favorite book read to you four times in a row? To have someone apply bug lotion, sun screen lotion, and kisses for boo-boos? To not have to worry about your weight, and for it to be CUTE when your tummy protrudes after a big meal?

Then again, can you imagine how frustrating it must be to not be able to get your shirt off and to always have to "wait a minute" before someone can help you? To be very thirsty, but have to wait for someone to supply the fluids? To want more than anything to wear the pink dress, when Mom insists on hand-me-down jeans, in case you get dirty? To entertain yourself quietly for an entire thirty minutes by drawing on walls, and get yelled at for your efforts? To "accidently" spill juice three times in one day, and get Mom grumpy like you did it on purpose? To need a quiet moment alone in your room, but not be allowed to climb the stairs?

Maybe thirty-something doesn't seem so bad after all.

Life with a newborn would be much easier if they could at least understand two things, "I'll be right back" and "Just a minute."

Last week my son was on top of a tire swing at a friend's house, while a much older boy sat safely in the tire, spinning them. Immediately, I envisioned the possible outcome of the situation, as I have done at least 200,000 times since becoming a mother. I saw him loosing his grip and falling backwards while still trying to hold on with his legs, his head hitting the ground below, causing injury to his neck and possible paralysis. He is still using his toddler swing for heaven's sake! Within 15 seconds I lifted him to safety while the other moms deemed me overprotective. Didn't they see what I saw? Maybe this 'what could happen' vision is more acute when it involves your own kids. My instinctive actions or decisions involving my children have never been altered on the chance I may be labelled overprotective.

Later that day, at home, my boy told me he didn't like being on top of the tire swing. Thank you, son.

What, I wonder, is the average number of days parents attempt to thoroughly answer their child's every "why?" before retreating peaceably to "because."

Some of my favorite mothering duties include re-tucking a sleeping child, rocking a sleeping baby, wrapping a shivering little wet one in a big bath towel, cuddling up for reading, hugging away the fear from a nightmare, applying magical kisses to boo-boos, being the reason for a smile, giving praise, saying yes.

Husband and son retire early. Daughter is dropped off at Grandma's. I start the car, headed for the Community College for my non-credit photography class. My sports car (which only moments ago was a family vehicle—never mind it still has two car seats occupying the back seat and toys on the floor—whizzes toward college. I smoothly shift gears as little puffs of dust roll off my back tires. I nonchalantly pop in a cassette (after I rummage through napkins, Wet Ones, and Raffi cassettes) and turn up the tunes—the Judd's singing *Girl's Night Out* and *Love Is Alive*. I sing along loudly, a carefree country singer on her way to a recording.

The car whisks around the college parking lot. I toss my camera bag and purse (with about twenty pictures of my kids in it) over my shoulder and clasp my portfolio (that sounds like a cool thing for a mother to be carrying). I confidently stroll toward class, skipping the elevator, lightly bounding up four flights of stairs. I am sure the young college boys are looking my way, instantly attracted to my woman-of-the-world appearance. I imagine for a brief moment I am childless, maybe even without husband. Will my Sesame Street bandaids blow my cover?

I find my class and sit down (for the third time since 5:45 am and this sit is to be gloriously longer than 2 minutes and 26–1/2 seconds . . . I don't even get up during breaks). For two hours I focus my thoughts on meters, depth of field, F-stops and shutter speeds. I ask woman-of-the-world questions demonstrating my knowledge and understanding of the presented material. Class is over—it goes quickly.

Back in the parking lot I fuddle through teething rings in my purse for my keys. I glance back at the car seats and feel lonely because they are empty. I drive the family car slower back to my parent's house to pick up my daughter. I get her home and to bed. My son gets a kiss on his sleeping

22

head. I am a woman of a home . . . a woman of a beautiful, loving family . . . just where I want to be.

Nursing my second has almost come to an end. We're down to once a day, actually once a night—a mere matter of convenience. So, I started consuming coffee again—real coffee—the stuff with zip. I feel like a kid in a candy store! It's a whole new life! It's a whole new energy! It's a whole new bounce! This feeling is so incredibly wonderful after getting up 2–4 times every night for the past seven months. I wonder how something so energizing can be legal and purchased on a grocery store shelf.

Love is playing and rewinding the same favorite song on cassette, as many times as they request, while riding in the car.

Things I have done for my three year old today include: filling his milk or juice cup about fourteen times; making his favorite lunch; taking his shirt off three times because it's the only part of dressing he still needs help with; tying his shoes at least four times; rescuing him from uncomfortable predicaments with his bike or booster chair because of his constant experimentation of alternative uses; letting him help me do the wash, vacuum, hang clothes on the line, do dishes, make cookies; retrieving three crayons and two Fisher Price people from under the refrigerator; kissing his boo-boos; reminding him to be gentle with his sister; washing his hair; reading him twelve books; telling him I love him and am proud of him at least four times; saying prayers at bedtime.

What, I wonder, will I do for him on a day when he is sixteen years old? Maybe . . . take him for a practice drive in preparation for his license, help him study for a test, wash a favorite shirt he needs to impress a girl, wash his sports uniform for practice or a game, remind him to put his clothes away and clean his room, and yes—it is his turn to do the dishes tonight, cook his favorite foods for supper, leave him a note somewhere to remind him I love him and am proud of him, remind him to not tease his sister, remind him not to read in bed too long, and hope he remembers to say his prayers before bed—or anytime.

The love I have for my children is the most powerful emotion I have ever experienced, a near-irrational love. After my first was born I confided rather guiltily to a very wise older woman that if something ever happened to my husband, devastation would engulf me, but I knew in time, a long time, I would heal. However, I felt if something happened to my child, I would never stop hurting, never stop feeling the pain that would forever be in my heart, and shattering my existence. She explained that my husband is a very important person in my life, but he is not my flesh and blood. My child is my flesh and blood. He is dependent on me for his daily existence; his whole well being; physically, spiritually, emotionally—his life. The thought is often overwhelming. When I think of it I hug my children a little tighter, and try even harder to be the best mom I can be.

My heart goes out to any woman, anywhere in the world, who has lost a child. I can't see that it would make any difference if the child had many siblings, or none; or if the child was less than an hour old, or forty. If it happened years ago, if it happened yesterday, I am so very sorry.

Anyone who works outside the home is somehow, at sometime evaluated by a superior. The evaluator usually praises good work or offers (hopefully) constructive criticism. Mothers only have each other. If a friend comments to another that she thinks she is a good mother, the glowing feeling lasts for a long time.

We recently asked friends to be guardians of our children. The mom told me how she was on a high for days afterwards from the honor, happiness, and excitement created from being told her mothering skills were so highly thought of.

A friend recently mentioned she was impressed with how I was with my son. I felt that happiness for days and can rekindle the feeling if I close my eyes and relive the moment, hear the words again. The words meant so much.

Mothering is hard work. It's so easy to let go, for a moment, of trying to be as perfect as you wish to be. If moms were told more often that their child raising techniques were highly thought of it would make the job easier during those trying times. We could puff our chests out and hold our chins high as we patiently clean up another milk spill, lovingly console one who has tears from yet another tumble, consistently discipline when necessary.

So, why don't we tell other moms what we think more often? This wonderful news is wasted if kept to ourselves! A simple "I think you're a good mom" would have such a warming and lasting effect. Let's try it, moms, you're doing great, keep up the good work!

Since becoming a parent I am amazed at the instructions I hear coming from my mouth. I always imagined, and expected, to utter instructions which included "crayons are for paper, not walls," "It's not polite to point," and "please chew with your mouth closed." However, I never expected to have to say "your buttered spaghetti is for eating, not for making bracelets," "no, you may not drink from the mud puddle like the dog, again," "please lick your cone from the top, don't bite off the bottom," and "PLEASE, don't lick the bird poop off your picnic table."

The love I feel for each of my two children is individual and special, but the strength and depth of passion is equal. Certainly one or the other may be more frustrating for an hour or require more attention, but I love them both with all my heart and soul. However, for a short time I could not say that.

My first child and I have been very close from his first breath. My husband has worked nights for a good part of Justin's three years; therefore, my son and I have greeted most mornings together and I have been the one to establish bedtime routines and tuck him in at night. We had an effective and comforting routine we liked to follow, with a change now and then to pamper a grumpy overtiredness or just for fun.

When I became pregnant a second time I was elated. To double the joy I had with my first was more than I could hope for. Justin was prepared from the moment my doctor confirmed our suspicions. He was almost two then and as excited about the news as his age could allow.

Preparing for a second child was quite different from the first, there was a little prince to plan into the event. I spent a lot of time thinking about appropriate "big brother" gifts. Four months prior to my due date we remodeled a new bedroom for our boy, complete with big bed. Everything seemed to be going smoothly. Then it hit me that I would be away overnight—actually two nights—when this next child decided to arrive. I had never been away from my boy all night. A home birth was suggested to my husband. He did not grab onto the idea. My mother, who lives close by, said she would be happy to care for Justin while I was away. Actually, she suggested the possibility of his sleeping over at their house. Was she crazy? My child had never slept away from his home overnight, and this was certainly not the time to start. I was already about to drastically change his life.

To help sooth my boy's time without me, many hours were spent compiling as accurate a description as possible of Justin's day: his routines, likes, dislikes, what it means if he says this, what to say if you want him to do that. The five page manual had to be updated several times before it was actually needed. Sometimes I would read the notes to my mom over the phone, just in case she had any questions. A tape was made of me saying things I knew would make him laugh and of me reading several of our favorite books, complete with "beeps."

Sometime during the last trimester, and admittedly a few times before, I began to remember what life with a newborn could involve. Thus, worry set in on different areas. Was this baby going to disrupt the schedule my prince and I had comfortably established? Suddenly the thought of this baby was not as thrilling as it had been earlier. Usually I felt we could handle anything—except, of course, any disturbance during our book reading time before bed. Our nightly fifteen to twenty books took us forty-five minutes to an hour. Because I worked full time for several months prior to maternity leave, this routine was important to me. The phone would get taken off the hook to avoid any disruptions during this special snuggle time.

My pregnancies are certainly uncomplicated, but my whole person simply does not care for the condition. My expanding belly began halting my carrying of heavy items, particularly my son up the stairs to bed. I began to miss carrying him. We did not even fit together in chairs and having him on my lap was certainly out of the question. It got difficult to tie his shoes, and mine. He had to climb into his car seat by himself. Of course, except for wanting me to carry him occasionally, Justin did not notice, or seem to mind these intrusions.

So, here we are, nine months pregnant with this baby who is sometimes in the way already. And I even discovered stretch marks! What a dark moment that was; Justin never gave me stretch marks! The worst was yet to come. My original due date was February 19th. The sonogram predicted the 14th. That was okay with me, the sooner the better. My son was four days early and a handleable 6 pounds 14 ounces. However, it did take 28 hours of labor before my womb would let him go. Well, the 14th came and went . . . the 19th came and went. I grew meaner and uglier by the day. I snapped at people who continually called to see if anything was going on. I felt mad at this baby before I even knew who it was. One day I confided to my husband that I did not like the baby. He was appalled. No one but a woman past her due date could ever understand. For necessary comfort and pampering I regularly visited sympathetic girlfriends, especially after uneventful doctor visits.

Then, on the morning of the 24th, I heavily sat my swollen body at the kitchen table to join my prince for breakfast.

"I feel so grumpy," I announced. He had heard that a few times before.

"Why, Mommy?" he asked. He had asked that a few times before.

"Because I want the baby to come out of my tummy today," I said, again.

"It will Mommy. The baby will come out today and it will be Rachel," he informed with confidence. He never changed his opinion on the sibling being Rachel, versus Caleb.

He was almost right. Labor started about 2:00 pm. After Justin was tucked in bed that evening contractions increased in frequency and intensity (first things first). My parents arrived. My husband and I left for the hospital. Contractions continued in the car—a good sign I decided. If we timed this right my husband could be home before Justin woke in the morning, a disappointing possibility to my mother.

Once I was comfortably strapped with monitors at the hospital, a pelvic exam was done. I imagined being at least 8 cm dilated. Why, this is a second child and they are supposed to come quicker, so I had been told. The verdict . . . 3 cm dilated. How can it be? I had been 3 cm for a month already!

At 3:00 am, now the 25th, I decided in all seriousness that it was time to go home to hug my boy. Every nurse had seen the two full mini albums of his pictures and had heard his life story, short as it was. Contractions had stopped. Frustration led to tears. I was sure of it now—I was to be ten months pregnant forever.

Finally my doctor arrived around 7:00 am. She ordered Pitocin to get things going. The stronger, more regular contractions were welcomed. With determined concentration I controlled each one with panting and breathing. My doctor commented "couple more good contractions and you can start pushing." This was so easy! Then I was told to push, but I didn't feel like pushing. Fun and easy took a flying leap out the window! Finally, at 11:45 am, after one hour and forty-five minutes of pushing and a few Tarzan screams, Rachel Rose was born, all 10 pounds 11–1/2 ounces of her. My husband marveled and wept upon her arrival, her beauty. He hugged her, he loved her from her very first breath. I did not, at least not like I thought I was supposed to.

She was late, she was big, she was swollen. I hurt, my bones were bruised, my legs shook, my throat hurt. The bonding just was not happening. She seemed like a stranger. I was afraid to tell anyone.

Rachel arrived at home. She was not an adored little baby, but an intrusion on my life with my prince. She kept me up all night so I had little patience or energy to offer Justin; she kept us from going outside at the drop of a hat; she cried while we read books.

One night during her first week, after being up until 2:00 am and having very little sleep in previous nights, I asked my husband, "Will I ever love her like I love Justin? Do you realize we have to keep her for the rest of our lives?" He calmly explained I was utterly exhausted. He reassured me I would feel better after I got some sleep. Fine, you breast feed her then.

Several times during Rachel's first few weeks I would hand her to her Daddy, "She needs burping and changing" I would inform him. "Justin and I are outa here." We would go do something very un-babylike such as playing basketball or going to the library. My husband could give her the one-to-one parent adoration I felt I could not do consistently.

Well, I can't say exactly when it happened, and it did relate to my hours of sleep, but little by little from Rachel's second week, I started loving her. Why she even offered things Justin could not, such as looking so beautiful in a dress (I never imagined getting so excited about miniature dresses, not being a big dress fan myself). She did not constantly require me to answer "why," or require any form of reasoning for that matter. She never squirmed to get down when I felt like cuddling. She let me rock her. She smelled that baby way. Despite what seemed like a rocky start, she loved me. Soon, I knew I loved my little girl. How special it was to have a daughter, a little princess.

Rachel did, and still does, cut our bedtime reading short. But Justin and I find other times to share books. Now we are enjoying a review of the board and plastic paged editions as we share our pleasure with our "little lady." We giggle at her actions and applaud her accomplishments. We are watching her grow together. Rachel has enhanced our family.

After all was calm and it was evident my love for Rachel was equal to the near irrational, crazy mother love I had for my son, I decided to ask girlfriends if they had loved their second child as quickly as their first. It was surprising and comforting to hear every mother's version; not one that I asked found the second time around to be as immediate. One mentioned looking forward to the baby's nap so she could cuddle her first born. One mom admitted to still not "connecting" with her second, even after several months.

At my six week postpartum check-up my obstetrician smiled and asked, "Are you going to keep her?" I answered affirmatively, but jokingly added the answer may have been different if posed a month earlier. After describing the feelings felt during those first weeks, she added that mothers simply do not have the time to get to know their second infant as quickly as their first because there is so much else taking up their time—mainly the first child. It takes awhile for things to settle down before mother and child can relax with each other. I mentioned it would have been easier for me if I had been more prepared, had read an article on the subject, that maybe I would write one to prepare another mom. She said there were articles on it, but to go ahead and write one . . .

My princess is almost eight months old now, and only if I really concentrate do I remember much of life without her; even the stretch marks have faded. Rachel, I'm so glad you are here. You have made me very happy.

It appears to be fairly universal: husbands are not awakened by the sounds of a child in the late p.m. or early a.m. hours. It amazes and frustrates me. One morning I recall clearly: husband stretches refreshed and says "he did great last night, didn't he" (referring to infant son). He receives an icy, exhausted stare and is informed that the child was up at 11:52, 2:17, and 4:26. (Aren't digital clocks a lifesaver? Now we know exactly how much sleep we're missing.)

Their condition is simply hard to relate to when we hear a child change their breathing pattern to signal an awake phase is coming. Many mornings the rustle of bed sheets awakens me before the child's verbal greeting to the morning.

I am going to warn my daughter about this someday, and be empathic to a daughter-in-law. And life, with sleep or without, goes on . . .

How many moms, like me, sometimes fall asleep while laying on their backs, only turning to a more comfortable sleeping arrangement after sleep takes over, in order to have both ears uncovered to better hear any sound from any child who may require tending to.

Microwave racing—the challenge of today. The goal is to see how much you can accomplish before the "beep, beep, beep." During a 15 second baby food warming I can get crackers, cheese (the string kind), carrots and celery sticks on a plate for a little person's lunch. During a 50 second run I can get all dirty dishes in or closer to the sink AND get any items requiring refrigeration in their proper place. Usually I can even pop the door before the third annoying "beep." The five second ice cream melt offers no challenge except to dash across the kitchen for a spoon, see how accurately I can count five seconds, or just watch the snack melt. But let's take a several minute dish . . . say, vegetables. In that six minutes I can set the table (including napkins), have hamburgers almost cooked, have all needed condiments on the table, and yes, still yes, pop the door before the third "beep". But, don't forget, I've been practicing.

Why, I have wondered, do they need three of those

beeps to let you know whatever is done, is done? I find the sound most obnoxious. To make matters worse they repeat the message every two minutes until you remove the contents. By that time the beeps talk to me, saying, "slow poke mama, hurry, hurry, hurry." I would pay good money for a microwave that had a recorded voice at the finale. It could sing "your delicious dish is ready you wonderful mommy, wonderful mommy, wonderful mommy."

The microwave's timer is almost always accurate. However, I have noticed a slow down time between 2:00 and 4:00 am; 45 seconds to warm a bottle for a baby who flatly refuses cold milk, seems more like 4 minutes and 50 seconds. Some night I will open my eyes, attempt to focus, and time it against another clock.

I challenge anyone in this new sport of microwave racing. I get faster and more efficient everyday. How disappointed I am when I race to the appliance only to still have seconds before the "beep." They are wasted seconds when something else could have been accomplished. With a little more practice (and I get lots of practice). I should be able to prepare an entire turkey dinner in the time it takes the scalloped potatoes to reach the third "beep". I may not be able to pop the door before the first message sounds, but I will retrieve the potatoes before the 2 minute warning. But then again, don't forget, I'm good.

Love is staying awake until 11:00 pm (when you were awakened at 5:00 am, when you really wanted/needed to retire at 9:00 pm) to tape Mary Poppins for the kids on the VCR . . . without commercials.

For my birthday I would like to take a nap. For Christmas I would like to sleep through the night—the whole eight hours worth. Sleep has definitely become a luxury item. My son did not sleep through the night consistently until he was seventeen months old. All I hoped for with the second was that it would be a better sleeper. She's not. If she only cries long enough for me to tend to her once, it's considered a good night. There have been exceptions. She has slept through five times now. Three of those nights my son decided to need me, on one of the nights the dog barked long and loud, and on the other there was a thunder storm. The end to sleepless nights does not appear to be in the immediate future, or even close.

Sometimes I take it personally. Sometimes I can understand I'm a mother of young children and a lack of sleep to tend to their nightly needs is part of the package. Sometimes I want to throw a tantrum and rip my hair out.

My husband's solution is always for me to go to bed right after they do (he works nights so is sleeping at this time). This is not possible because the house turns completely to shambles as I concentrate on their bedtime routines. Also, once they're in bed I cherish my few hours alone. No one is asking me questions, requiring me to speak, or dictating my direction. How can I give that up—even for precious sleep?

Well, my breast feeding experience has ended for the second time, maybe the last. Nursing is so individual, some women love it, some women hate it. Some babies love it, some babies hate it. Some breasts love it, some breasts hate it.

My son was nursed for six months. It wasn't easy. He refused my offer for sustenance for three days before taking me seriously. It was 3:00 am on a Sunday when he finally nursed both sides in one feeding. I woke my husband to share the good news. He sleepily muttered, "good work, Justin." Hey, what about me?

Justin was full after five minutes on one side. Then for awhile he refused my left side causing a lopsidedness to my figure. Every time I grocery shopped while he stayed with Grandma, my milk would come in at the diaper aisle. Leakage was a problem until I drank fewer liquids than was recommended. Some people could not understand breast milk was all the child needed to survive the first months, so explanations were necessary. Because Justin was so plump on so little milk, I was compared to a cow that is known to have a high fat content in their milk . . . moo. None of my shirts fit. I smelled like sour milk. It did not help me lose weight any faster. And what about bedtime wear? Our upstairs is seasonally cold which mandates long flannel shirts and sexy sweatpants with wool socks. I cannot be expected to dress in the dark at early morning hours, comfort is a main concern! Finally, by six months, I called it quits. A medal should be awarded for such efforts!

My daughter showed more promise. She demonstrated the rooting reflex within seconds after delivery, while her Daddy was holding her. She nursed heartily right away. What a relief, this was going to be different! Right. Rachel wanted to nurse every moment, of every hour, during every evening. My breasts would be engorged by morning, but she would not display an appetite for my beverage until I was quite uncomfortable. Finally, she took a pacifier. But then she became a five minute nurser, too, except of course in the middle of the night when I had to rip myself from her suction to get away. When she got more alert she would forget to loosen her grip when she turned her lips 180 degrees to catch some action. Then started the games—a sip here, a smile there, for the duration of dinner. If I wanted to continue nursing her I would have to spend feeding time upstairs in a dark closet. I gave in—it happened again at six months.

Breast feeding . . . I'm glad I did it . . . I'm glad it's over.

Language must be very confusing to children. They learn the meaning and usage of an idea or word one day only to have it mean something else the next. It must take years to figure it all out.

Take, for example, teaching green means go. This fact of life was a topic of discussion during car rides with my son before his vocabulary was very extensive. It was evident he had been listening when later from his high chair perch, he shook his dill pickle spear at me and proclaimed "go, go, go."

Another confusing area has been with petting animals. For months he would "pet" family members and friends. When we were introducing the idea of a new baby in the house he reassuringly said he would "pet the baby so soft."

And what about turtle necks? We take the description for granted, not realizing the confusion it could cause. One morning my son was trying to tell me what he wanted to wear for the day. I admitted to not understanding his description. Finally, he confidently smiled and informed "a frog neck, Mommy. I want to wear a frog neck."

The other day I shared in Justin's excitement over the dollar his Papa had given him. "I know what we can buy with that . . . " I hinted. "Paints?" shrieked Justin. "Yes!" I exclaimed. "We'll run to the store tomorrow and get them!" He was picturing this . . . "can't we ride in the car?"

It is encouraged in this household to stop eating when you feel full. Justin arose even earlier than usual one day last week, so I talked him into getting into bed with me, hoping to catch 15 minutes more shut eye. "But I'm full of sleep," he complained. How can I argue with that line of reasoning?

A few nights ago, as it approached bedtime, Justin asked "Is it time to hit the sack?" I smiled and said yes it was. Since I am the one who puts him to bed he must have heard me use the phrase. I doubt it was used too many times, but he sure remembered. Now as I think about it, it sounds like a very silly thing to say. I wonder what the words mean to him.

Another evening, while Justin was in the tub and Rachel was finishing supper in her high chair, I decided to sing a new song to entertain them until I could finish dishes. "On Top Of Spaghetti" was my choice—I could have done better. As I ended with "so hold on to your meatball and don't ever sneeze," I laughed and asked Justin if he thought it was funny. He was not laughing.

"What happened to the meatball, Mommy?" he inquired from the bath tub with a serious tone.

"It rolled off the table."

"Oh. And it is mush, why?"

"Because it rolled under a bush."

"Oh. Sing it again. Mom, from the beginning." It was going to be a long time before he found the humor in this one.

Does every child first translate Winnie-the-Pooh to Winnie-the-Poop?

Why is a teeter-totter also a see-saw? What do children think when they are first told someone is crying because they are so happy?

Nursery rhymes sometimes contradict what we teach him. It has always been important to us for Justin to understand he is always a good boy. He sometimes does naughty things, but he is not a naughty boy. Then we came across the Mother Goose tale that includes "Ding, dong bell, pussy's in the well . . . what a naughty boy was that to try and drown poor pussy cat . . . " Okay, so let's not dwell on it, just turn the page. But of course it's the one he wants to hear again and again.

What has also gotten me into trouble before is "hold your horses!"

"My horses, Mommy?" He looks at me like I have lost my mind.

"Never mind, just slow down."

"What horses, Mommy?"

"Forget I said it." It's best to change the subject as quickly as possible.

Or how about "No way, Jose."

"I'm Justin," he insists, "don't call me Jose." Sorry son, it just didn't have the same swing.

Yesterday, my son once again begged for a cookie too near a mealtime. I felt a need to discuss good and bad things we can do to our bodies. Good being healthy foods and exercise, bad being too much sugar . . . It was obvious Justin was wrestling mentally with something when he finally added "and it's not good when people suck fire, huh, Mom?" After an instant of confusion I burst into laughter, much to his amusement. Cigarette smoking has taken on a whole new look for me.

Our language is a funny thing to learn, but as long as we keep talking, our kids are sure to figure it out. It's interesting being the teacher when the student keeps teaching back what you really mean. At least there's plenty of giggles along the way.

I came home from my one hour a week break, I mean job, to two exhausted kids and a hungry husband. What to do first? (I am often confronted with that question.) Older child can be kept busy by letting him help me get lunch ready. Hungry husband to hold younger child until her cereal with bananas can be prepared. Also, there is a need to fix another lunch for older child because he would rather starve than eat what I (we) are preparing.

Okay, children are fed. Older child up for a nap. Oh, no, he is at that "I don't want my blankie. I don't want my Baby Puppy" stage of exhaustion which means he'll be refusing these items now, crying for them later. I leave him in his room, hoping he'll settle down. I add an ingredient to cooking lunch and tend to younger child.

She nurses a bit, but refuses to settle down. Older child is crying for something. Hungry husband tends to him—a hundredth hug was needed, a bee in his room was killed. Okay, he should settle down now. Still working on the blankie, Baby Puppy situation.

How's lunch . . . is it burning? It smells done, but it's simply out of my reach.

Younger child down to play, to exert energy, making sleep easier.

Older child fussing, again. I'm desperate for a moment's peace so I try "If I have to come up there again, I'm going to spank you." There, that should work. It doesn't work. I go up; tearfully he says he needs a hug. Well, first a spank so I can be one of those moms who carries through with what she says then a hug. There, now I feel good and guilty, even though it was no more that a pat, even though it worked.

Back to younger child who is now crying. Good, energy level reduced to that required for napping. Finally, she's asleep.

After twenty minutes of the quiet my appetite returns for lunch. Husband has already eaten. He comments on the quiet.

Today is one of those wonderful days when a mom, who I felt a bit awed by because I think she's a perfect mother who never loses her patience with her kids, tells me she loses it with her kids. Yes! It's also a terrific thing to awe somebody else because they think I'm that perfect one. I'm always a bit disappointed, yet relieved, when I spill the beans. But I never realize they thought this of me until after I share a grisly moment from our household. Oh, well, I made it a wonderful day for them.

When my husband and I started our family we began to sort through our childhoods from our earliest memories to our present parent relationships. We more and more frequently discussed our likes and dislikes of our parents' actions and decisions and how we feel they affected us then and today. We recognized actions we respected and agreed with and try to include those actions in our parenting techniques. We recognized actions we disagreed with and make an effort to not include them in our parenting styles.

All of this leads me to wonder: what will my children like or dislike, agree with or disagree with, about how they are being raised? What will they decide to include with their parenting styles? What will they decide over coffee with their spouse, not to include in raising their own children?

He's ready for "lunch" and asks to eat in the family room because he can't tear himself from Sesame Street.

Great, I'll feed her.

She's in the swing eating prunes.

She sneezes prunes all over me.

She's tired, but won't rock to sleep. He's playing and continuously demands me to "look, Mom" at every creation and accomplishment. I'm feeling impatient so put her in playpen to amuse herself.

I tell him it's time to read books. He's ready.

I pick her up to join us.

Uh-oh, poops.

He can play with pennies while I change her. Okay, she's changed. Let's go read books. He wants to finish what he started. I want kids in bed.

Me—"I'm starting *The Truck Book* now."

He—"I'm coming. I'm coming."

Me—"Trucks dump gravel and pull logs . . . ."

He—"I'm coming. I'm coming."

Finally, he comes.

Several pages read, several to go . . . we're relaxed. She starts to fuss.

She's banging the pages of our book.

She won't be distracted with a toy.

She pokes his eye.

He gets up to get her a book she can chew on. We're reading again.

There, all books read.

She to playpen.

He to bed with blanket.

Once upstairs, he wants milk. I say no, guiltily. Hugs. Kisses.

Back to her. I pull rocking chair over by television, my entertainment until she's asleep. It keeps me awake. My time for me is coming . . . it's coming. If I can stay awake . . . it's coming.

She loses pacifier twice. It goes under a chair—this mandates rinsing.

We're settled rocking.

The last ten minutes of 60 Minutes seems interesting . . . her sleepy-song drowns out 75% of the words. She's asleep. The show's over.

I hug and kiss her to ensure good dreams (and maybe a possible sleep through).

He's still awake. I get him some milk. There, guilt over. Me relaxing.

He cries a bit.

I check.

He can't find his "Baby Puppy."

I retrieve him from the sheets.

More hugs. More kisses.

Soon, they're both asleep.

My time alone has arrived. What shall I do first?

This has been an exciting week! My boy started Sunday School and Story Hour. He enjoys them thoroughly and voices his thoughts: "I'm excited to go to Sunday School, Mom!" I'm bursting with excitement and pride for him. Does everyone notice my beam? Part of me wants him to cling a bit more, but most of me is comfortable letting go. An hour here . . . an hour there . . . with pre-school next year he just may have me ready for Kindergarten. But, I doubt it.

Our bodies seem to fight so letting them go from the womb, and it never really stops.

Have you ever had a discussion with your husband where you eventually say, "But my job is twenty-four hours a day, seven days a week!" with the emphasis on twenty-four and seven? And then you most likely said at one point, "I'd just like to see you do what I do for a day!" I have a difficult time believing my husband has a hard day at work; why he didn't have the kids to watch while he was there!

Moms just don't get enough breaks. Whenever I leave the house I feel more comfortable, less guilty, if I have one child with me, to relieve any stress on the home front in my absence. Or, I race away while one child is napping, often with a child still with me. (As I read this several months later I realize the greater ease on which I leave the house alone. It must have to do with the kids being older.) Why don't we allow ourselves more breaks? After my first child was born I didn't want to admit I needed one. It was only an unfit mother who would ever request a moment's time away from her child, her own flesh and blood. I mean, for heaven's sake, the child didn't ask to be here. The evening always seemed to revive me for the next day as I covered him, quiet and still at last. As I stared at his angelic little face I lost the urgency for a break I felt just a few hours earlier.

Now, after my second, I'm not only more apt to ask

for a break, but I ask for it in a near hysterical manner. "If I don't get a break soon I'm going to drop our children off at the nearest house and go shopping with the VISA card!" This usually gets things going.

More on taking a break from mothering. Do other mothers feel much more relaxed if they wait to leave the house after all children are tucked in and sleeping soundly? How does this count as a break if you would be alone anyway? Just recently I have convinced myself to not feel too terribly guilty in leaving Daddy or Grandma with a meal to prepare and serve, or even a nap to negotiate. It's amazing how smoothly things go in my absence. It's amazing how an hour or two break prepares me for anything the kids can dish out for another week or two. It's amazing I don't do it more often. We mothers are such troopers.

Have you ever noticed how the father of the children can announce nonchalantly he's going outside to work in the garden, mow the lawn, change the oil in the car, or chop wood. Off he goes with no child in tow. If I go outside it's after he's gone potty, after I've put on three pairs of shoes and appropriate outer wear, after I've opened the stroller and filled it with toys, after I've changed a diaper or fastened the nursery monitor somewhere on myself. What would happen if I tried his method of exit? And the men actually think it's work they're doing, at least that's what my husband claims. I remember mowing the lawn b.c. (before children) when we still had the push mower—it was fun! I just may discover where the car's oil plug is tomorrow.

During my first pregnancy I remember worrying about how this family addition would effect the idealistic relationship my husband and I shared. We were the mushy kind—several phone calls during the day, picnic lunches together during warm weather (our work places were close). After work we would eat together then work in our gardens, waving hello every now and then. If I really concentrate I can remember enthusiastic viewings of college basketball games. I worried that my expanding belly would cause his eye to wander. He would come home and tell me I looked even more beautiful. I recall telling my husband he would always come first. This promise lasted about thirty seconds after Justin's birth.

During labor for our boy, in the 28th hour as my eyes again rolled back in exhaustion, my husband promised, "When this is over I am going to pamper you for the rest of your life." No kidding? Justin and I arrived home to an immaculate house (wasn't it always like that before children, my memory is foggy). My husband continued to do all meal preparation, laundry, dishes, shopping, and cleaning—for one week. I guess he kept his promise longer than I did mine.

The second pregnancy found me angry at my husband. I reminded him often of the discomforts of my condition (by the book I had easy pregnancies) and of his measly contribution to the whole thing, one lousy sperm, and that donated by means of ecstasy. Things just didn't quite balance. And to make matters worse, the husbands never seem to supply the necessary pampering in any pregnancy after the first.

Just for fun let's chart this out:

Daddy's donation: one sperm.

Mommy's donation: egg, uterus and other delicate anatomical features, morning sickness, weight gain, hemorrhoids, swelling, nausea, stretch marks, LABOR, stitches, eliminating caffeine-artificial sweeteners-alcohol, up nights for what could be the rest of our lives.

And this is only a rough listing!

Have you ever said, "we'll have another baby when you can have it." Bet they'd rather mow the lawn. Bet they'd rather mow a whole lot of lawns!

But, just between you and me, sometimes I miss being pregnant and that exciting anticipation of what's to come. And I wouldn't trade the unique opportunity to experience being such a part of the miracle of birth for anything in the world . . . once of course I've lost all the weight from this last miracle.

We haven't decided positively if we'll have more children. Usually the idea of being pregnant again and making it through those initial stages of major household disruption do not excite me, especially now that things are going smoothly from our last change in family dynamics. Also, I feel so busy in meeting the needs of the two children entrusted to me now, I don't feel I could possibly be the kind of mom I want to be with another child to care for.

But, I know as my two children grow and have less immediate needs for me to tend to I may think more about it. Sometimes, on especially good days, I already do. Sometimes the thought of another little being around to feel this incredible love for is even quite strong, although short lived at this point.

And then there are those special one-per-child moments I'll daydream of reliving. To some it may be the first smile, tooth, step or word. The most special moment to me is the moment of birth, the first breath; the moment you discover if the baby you've been carrying is a boy or girl. The bundle looks at you for the first time, now named, and welcomed to the world. There is no other child in the world like him, or her; a being only possible because of you and your partner's combination. And there's the vow to do your very best for this tiny, totally dependent new person only minutes old. Yes, that's the moment I'll miss the most or be excited to live again.

And just for the record, right up there with favorite moments is the emergence of those front two top teeth.

Every once in a while during the late afternoon I feel a bit frustrated because it seems I haven't accomplished anything. There's been no wash done, cookies baked, projects completed, sweat from exercise, or a major house part cleaned. Even if the grocery shopping took place, it never seems to count, maybe because it happened so many hours ago.

But then I remember to include important tasks (if that be the accurate description) playing with, reading to, being a mom to my kids. A feeling of warm satisfaction replaces frustration as I mentally make a list of the day's accomplishments: filled kid's bellies, companion to kids, kid's had a wonderful day. Everything else will have to work around that, or wait.

We must create a more efficient method in this house of giving certain instructions, demands that require repeating so many times in a day that one finds their throat sore, their voice gone, or temporary insanity threatening.

After a bit of thought, I decided against the sign approach, (although sign language seemed like a good possibility) and go with the "beep" system. Let me be more specific:

One "beep" from a parent means "Please close the door! The bugs are coming in!"

Two "beeps" means "The couch is for sitting on!"

Three "beeps" means "Remove your hands from your sibling, or pay the consequences!"

Four "beeps" means "Please close the refrigerator door, the milk is going to get warm!"

Five "beeps" means "In a minute!"

Do you get the idea? I'm sure every family has their own needs on what each "beep" would mean. There are a number of possible methods, but I decided the simpler the better. Hmmmm . . . then again, maybe dance steps would work . . . think of the exercise we'd get!

When parents mention that these infant, toddler, pre-school years are easy compared to adolescent, teenage years . . . when they suggest that being up every night, dirty diapers, potty training, "NO," endless filling of tip-it cups, dressing, making sandwiches, tying shoes, answering countless "Why's," brushing teeth, trimming nails, washing faces, and fastening of car seat buckles is the <u>easy</u> part, there's only one thing I have to say:

"AAAAAAAAAAGGGGGGGGGGHHHHHHHHHH!"

This Christmas season finds me even more choosy in selecting gifts for my three year old. Past Christmas and birthday choices have proved to me the more imagination a toy allows, the more popular it will be. Small houses, barns, or towns have been less popular than a set of blocks for making his own miniature constructions. Expensive peg boards were less exciting than an old shoe box with clothespins all around. Coloring books are used so little in comparison to the piles of plain white construction or bond paper used for painting, cutting, stenciling, coloring, markers, or storywriting. With all the name brand toys my son has he chooses to spend a surprising number of hours making designs with dog biscuits on the kitchen floor, clipping clothespins to a tree, playing with cups in a sink filled with water, or writing stories in an old date book I was ready to throw away.

So, this Christmas I am choosing gifts wisely. The simpler, the better. I won't go so far as to get him his own box of dog biscuits; I'm still contemplating stuffing his stocking with his own set of colorful clothespins; but I won't forget a very tall stack of plain white paper.

Mothers are the busiest people I know. Stay-at-home moms wonder how those who work full time outside the home do it. Career oriented moms wonder how stay-at-home moms do it. Part time working moms either feel they have it made or wish they were one of the other two. I always felt too busy to go back to work after having a baby and shuddered at the thought of working anything else into what seemed like an already overloaded day. But, whatever landed in my path seemed to fit in my schedule for as long as it had to.

Some things have to go for any and all moms. All the books say this, but I never believed them, before children.

For me it has been the kitchen floor. Sometimes I wonder if it'd be easier if we just tore it up and left the dirt there to rake, but I would never find time to even smooth it over. Also, I only turn my husband's T-shirts right side out if I'm having an unusually calm moment at the time they require folding. Do you still fold underwear and socks? My children's clothes make it to their proper place and my husband somehow gets his things put away, but I live out of a clothes basket, wearing the same thing everyday until I take a moment to paw through a rumpled dresser drawer for something new. Hangers are my pet peeve; life is too short to spend so much time trying to get them to work right. My husband mounted a large peg board on our bedroom wall so I'd at least hang some articles on that. I usually find time to throw things on a peg, but if it doesn't stay after two tries, it stays floored.

Reading is something I miss. After becoming a mother, if I was to read during daylight hours, I'd choose a book with short chapters or separate paragraphs like the short humor blurbs at the end of articles in The Reader's Digest. I could usually get in a few of those. Now I simply don't attempt reading adult material (you know—the newspaper, *Parents* magazine, the book club order) until all children are asleep. This way I avoid reading the same line eleven times in order to be ready for the next sentence. Sometimes my strong desire to read gets stressful. Just when I feel I'm under control, having read some of the majority of things I want to skim, I'll get a magazine in the mail. Instead of the usual elation at the thought of reading new information, I feel threatened that this assortment of pages will get me behind again.

Eating is another major area of change since children. I fantasize about eating out without children, or in the least, a quiet meal at home while they're both asleep. My husband and son have a similar condition: they both become very talkative in the car and at the dinner table. They both want me to listen and neither hears the other. Meanwhile I'm concentrating on everything being cooked to an edible degree, feeding the one in the high chair, trying to avoid crunching every Cheerio on the floor, refilling milk cups, cleaning up spills, and keeping hot things in a safe place. I usually sit down to eat panting, with everyone else nearly finished. Many times a napkin is thrown over my meal, laying it to permanent rest, or preparing it for the microwave at a much later time. Sometimes I choose my food by how long it has to be chewed. Sometimes supper consists of peanut butter sandwich crusts, left over baby oatmeal with peaches, or cold alphabet pasta. And, if someone is due to wake up from a nap, all I have to do is sit down to eat for it to happen.

Love is removing the third pair of muddy wet pants from a cold wet body on the first warm spring day, with a smile on your face and the washing machine door open.

Kindergarten teacher was my profession for 1–1/2 years between children. I felt effective in that my students loved coming to school. Teaching is very important to me; it was difficult to resign to be home during my kid's very early years, but I feel thankful I've had the chance.

The school district I taught at, and hope to return to, is where my children will attend. It's still a few years away, but I know the first day will be traumatic for me. The part I look forward to is the preparation: buying new clothes, a pencil case, a lunch box, a pack to carry projects safely home in. The fun ends there.

As long as Kindergarten remains half day things should be okay, but they keep pushing for full day here. As a teacher I can readily recognize its benefits; as a mother I can readily recognize its drawbacks. As a teacher I can realize it is a terrific situation for some kids; as a mother I am not at all interested in having my children away from me all day at such a tender age.

Age five is too young to be away from home all day. A five year old needs to eat his lunch in a quieter place than those obnoxious cafeterias. A five year old needs a rest time in a relaxed, familiar place. A five year old needs the love, hugs, and kisses of his mother if he is hurt or sad . . . and he's bound to get hurt or sad if he's away all day.

A teacher simply cannot provide the necessary mothering that is required of twenty, or more, five year olds . . . well, my five year old. (Does it make any difference that I think I could come close as a teacher?)

Actually, he says he is looking forward to school . . . maybe it's me. I'm just glad it's still a few years away.

Religion has always been wonderfully simple for me. It's been a "Jesus loves me this I know" sort of relationship. It has been the loveliest thing teaching my son what I believe. We've covered the "all things bright and beautiful . . . " areas. He knows God made everything in the natural environment. He asked me once "who made Justin?" I reminded him Mommy and Daddy did. He reminded me "and God, Mommy."

We began prayers at a young age, maybe two-ish. They were simple: "Dear Jesus, thank you for the day. Bless Mommy, Daddy . . . and everybody else." One evening he began with "Dear Jesus, welcome to Sesame Street." Knowing his love for the show at the time, it was a real compliment.

Many times he'll come up with something that makes me smile so, that reminds me of how beautifully simple faith can be. I asked him once who he was going to marry. His usual "Mommy" response was changed to "Jesus". Wouldn't that be something! Maybe Jesus is a woman . . . did I ever mention to him that Jesus was most likely a man? He's already coming up with his own answers.

His attendance at Sunday School has reinforced and broadened what we attempt to teach at home. He relates his understanding of the material at unexpected times. One day I confided to him I wasn't myself because of a tummy ache.

He responded "I will always be with you even when you are sick." The words had a familiar ring, so I tested "who else is always with you?" Without a moment's hesitation he announced "God is" proving the value and importance of the Sunday School's lessons and teachers.

Recently, out of the blue, he shared what was on his mind "God is magic." I hesitated on my response not yet ready to completely accept that concept. Why magic isn't real, but God's works are true, not a game with our vision. But after a moment I felt it was a grand way of viewing the Lord's works, especially through the eyes and thoughts of a three year old. I agreed with him with strong confidence. "God is magic" is on my mind a lot these days. I find the concept quite comforting at times. It didn't take many lessons before my son gave one of his own.

Heaven has been our latest topic in the Christian area. I told him of a friend's grandfather dying and going to heaven, attempting to leave it as simple as possible, only answering his questions until he felt satisfied. The point must have gotten through. Justin was informed that our "red car" couldn't be fixed, it had died. "Is it going to heaven, Mommy?" I confided that cars weren't needed in heaven because I thought maybe when you got there some type of wings were placed on your backs so you could fly around if you wanted. "I think maybe you are right, Mommy." I hope I am.

Sometimes I feel like reading a book, writing a poem, exercising, calling a friend, writing a letter, reading the paper, playing the piano, going shopping for something other than food, eating uninterrupted, taking a nap, weeding my garden, putting my feet up, talking to a grown-up about life.

But I have to change a diaper, cook a meal, sweep up Cheerios, kiss a boo-boo, do the laundry, take clothes off the line, put clothes away, wash dishes, put dishes away, pack a lunch, vacuum crumbs, give a bath, tie a shoe, clean up spilled milk, talk about Big Bird to a little person.

Today I did three extra large loads of wash, got what would fit on the line placing every available clothes pin in a strategic place (I always enjoy this challenge), then it rained . . . and rained . . . and rained. Some days I stand my ground and refuse to remove the clothes from their position until they're finally dry. But today I had to admit defeat, haul every last article inside to be put through another spin cycle before throwing them in the dryer. It just takes the punch out of the hour.

When we needed a change in books from our everyday favorites, Justin and I looked through our own library's children's shelf and came up with *The Little House*, by Virginia Lee Burton. The story is lovely, but was too long for his two year age, so I ad-libbed here and there finally reaching the end, and glad of it. Best to put this one back on the shelf for another few months, I thought. But Justin wanted to hear it again, and again. We simplified the story to a house loving its country location, then feeling sad about her eventual change to city life, making for a happy ending. Unbeknownst to me, Justin was listening, grasping the message in his own way, and ready to apply the concept where he saw fit.

It was Thanksgiving. We were preparing for a visit with family. I don't recall the details that led to my state of frustration. Pregnancy was in its sixth month, so maybe that was part of it. Anyway, Justin found me sitting on the floor crying. He asked me what was wrong. I explained I just felt a little sad. This concerned him so he brought his little white chair close, positioning it directly in front of me, despite his father advising him to leave me alone. I liked the attention. His serious look told of his thought patterns in steady motion. Finally, he asked, "Do you live in the city, Mommy? And you want to live in the country?" With a smile I reassured him our home in the country was just where I wanted to be and it's okay to be sad sometimes.

My lesson was simple: reading books with your children is worth more than one knows.

Being a mother allows me to participate in activities

I thoroughly enjoy, activities that might otherwise be considered quite immature for my age. Participation in these activities would cause quizzical looks or giggles if I weren't a mom; however, because of my status of mother the participation is deemed appropriate, even complimentary.

Coloring, for example, is one of my favorites. Justin and I color together while discussing favorite hues and showing off our creations. Sometimes he colors on my side. I mind, but usually don't say anything. He is more apt to choose less traditional colors, like periwinkle or copper, while I almost always find myself with one of the eight primary styles. Although, burnt orange can be found more often in my drawings lately. Justin does not mind at all how much the point is worn down; however, I find myself drawn to the newer looking color stick, if there's a choice. The smell of crayons is intoxicating to me. I would wear perfume if they could make one that smelled similarly. Often while I am running around picking up the house I will take a break to smell the crayons. It's a real pick-me-up! We have hundreds of crayons, but recently added a new box of 64 count Crayolas to the pile to see what those new colors were like. That was an exciting day.

Stomping in puddles is another activity I feel free to engage in. Why, just today the kids and I could be found at the puddle end of the driveway stomping in and splashing through the water patches. Rachel participated by being pushed through the deepest part while sitting in her stroller. After a while we searched for big stones to throw in for ripple effects. During the wettest seasons we have what we call "the pond" beyond the driveway. When we moved to this home, then childless, my husband suggested we have the low area filled in, but I saw endless possibilities for the large puddle and insisted it not be disturbed. Sure enough, it's to a depth at certain times that requires pants to be rolled to the knees. There are even tadpoles to watch turn into frogs. (My husband has even been known to fill the puddle from the hose if necessary, to save the tadpoles.) Puddles are wonderful things.

Painting is new in this house since Christmas. Sure, we've had waterpaints, but Tempera paints are a different story! The only colors left at a local preschool were violet and magenta. The house is covered with two colored creations. Needless to say we are eagerly anticipating the addition of other colors. Anyway, watching Justin form endless smiling suns, clouds, boats, and other designs with these brilliant hues was more than I could stand. He gave me permission to share his brushes and paints one afternoon. How excited I was to begin! I pondered over what to create, then I had it! I would make my very own robot, an idea from a book we had been reading together. It was beautiful—a "Loving (it had a heart shaped head) Three Belly Buttoned Purple Toe Nailatron." Justin made suggestions as to hair color, then created his own "Pink Purple Pink Android—who is walking" (the knees bent—a first for him!). He asked if he could hang mine up in his room! I was bursting with pride, it is the FIRST painting to be hung in our upstairs, thank you very much.

There are many more examples I could discuss, I wouldn't want you to get bored. One thing is for sure, being a mom has given me the chance to be a kid and the tools to do it with. As long as the kid in me stays alive, I should be okay.

The environment and its maintenance have always been important to me. This attitude is infectious; Justin commented the other day "I don't want the earth to get dirty." I had no idea what was said to trigger this comment. I explained matter-of-factly that I felt the same way and we were doing what we could to keep it clean. His awareness is important, but I didn't want him to dwell on it to a worry degree at his age.

Recycling was explained simply, old stuff to new stuff. We talked more often about whether an item was appropriate for the process at home. He understood. One day, after he had collected a wagon load of pinecones, I inquired as to what he planned to do with then all. "Make new pinecones from the old ones, Mom!" Of course!

We make every attempt to buy our eggs at the local grocery store to avoid the styrofoam packaging. Everytime, without fail, he asks "these eggs help keep the earth clean?" What magical eggs they would be! My explanation on packaging may not be wholly understood, yet.

He understands a bit about waste, too. After using a paper towel to clean up a milk spill, he set it down assuring me we could use it again before throwing it away. Lately, he has been known to put any plastic wrap removed from a leftover snack back on the counter rather than in the garbage.

When we walk down the lane between the fields he insists on putting any paper or plastic found in his sister's stroller basket, to be thrown away at home. When we walk through a parking lot he wants us to pick up the garbage in our path on the way to the store. In this case I explain, for sanitary reasons, that it's someone else's job to clean up the parking lot, although I feel a twinge of guilt at the inconsistent message.

My son developed this desire to help keep the earth clean rather quickly, devotedly, enthusiastically. If everyone supplied their three year olds with the basic information, the earth could be in very good hands.

I know it's going to be a long day when I look at the clock to count the hours until bedtime and it's only 9:00 am.

Before I was a mother I would have thought any woman who talked of crying just because their child turned one year of age, needed psychiatric help. Well, sign me up. The urge to cry uncontrollable sobs was with me all day when my son turned one. Having family there to share in the celebration helped in maintaining control.

The fact the day even arrived is proof time is not standing still—they are going to get older whether we like it or not. If they can turn one on us, that means they will someday insist on being five and put us through a first day of Kindergarten . . . they will someday turn eighteen and want to actually leave us to attend college. If our children learn to walk and talk, that means they will someday learn to read and no longer need to be read to. Someday they will move their belongings to their own home and we'll have to share in being so important in their lives. Day by day . . . hour by hour . . . minute by minute . . . our children get older. Somehow that first birthday seems to be the point of no return.

We have another one coming up in our house . . . and I never really expected to cry.

Strange sounds are heard when I take a shower. I hear someone breaking into the house, the furnace blowing up, a child crying, a child calling "Mommy!" When I peek my dripping head out to listen: silence. Who can explain it?

Today was fun. You cannot detect the sarcasm in this message because you're reading; please note appropriate tone. My children lost their sense of understanding that Mom is Ruler. They lost all previously learned skills in the listening area.

Every request I made, every command uttered, had to be repeated three times. It seems "Don't do that" meant "Do it again, only harder;" "Please be quiet" meant "Do it again, only louder;" "Pick that up" meant "Scatter them first so the picking up takes longer." By the late afternoon I had it down—without looking, I could relay messages in three words each: "No, No, NO!"

The only thought that got me through until bedtime was knowing the day's events could be written down. This reminded me that somewhere in the world another mom was experiencing a similarly fun day. What a valuable thought it was, for it brought on a giggle or two to end our day.

One of the hard parts about being a mom is displaying delight and appreciation for the 43rd dandelion given within the span of three hours time.

As the supper hour began, I felt a strong case of the grumpies arriving; it was evident from the difficulty I seemed to be having in getting my lips to form a happy expression. My voice was beginning to resemble a bark. The previous nights lack of sleep, including a middle of the night crib change, was surely the cause, but it was important to get the kids to bed with thoughts closer to sugar plums, rather than witches, dancing in their heads.

Justin was put in the tub with a popsicle of his favorite color and lots of toys. Rachel was generously given a few ounces of milk in her "ba-ba" and positioned in her playpen to rely on Mr. Rogers for entertainment. I hesitated in my retreat when I passed through the kitchen and sight fixed on the mess left from supper not yet tackled, but first things first I reminded myself.

The nursery is my hideout on such occasions. I lie on the floor to feel that most loved position—horizontal—and prop my feet up on an unopened bag of diapers. With my eyes closed I can get a proper perspective on the evening's events, and a bit of rest, to see me through until they're asleep. The nursery is next to the bathroom, and only a room away from the playpen, but it separates me from them long enough for my sense of humor to take over in the few hours left before they're tucked in. The moment may last just that, or sometimes my physical self remains off duty for several more, but it's a better person who responds to the inevitable "Mommy!"

Women who are not mothers are missing out on some very exciting moments. How can we explain the thrill of walking the entire length of the kitchen floor without crunching a Cheerio, walking from one room to another without stepping over a gate, finding something still clean after an hour's time, lying in a horizontal position, a good night's sleep, a quiet moment, a moment alone.

My kids get away with more when I'm desperate to have one more minute to finish something, or when I need, just for a minute, to not say "No". This has included the kids emptying a cupboard of baking pans, assorted sauce pans with lids, and other items, creating a disturbance that makes me appreciate our country existence; having dessert before the meal; having the glue and glitter without my presence;

watching a cartoon station on the television; playing with Daddy's socket set while sitting on the dryer; or maybe wading in puddles on a day colder than what makes this activity appropriate. The difficulty comes when Daddy catches us in the act. I try my best to explain, "but he is HAPPY," or "but it is giving me a MOMENT'S peace." Daddy is reminded of these instances after I catch him attempting the same.

Life is too short to worry about wearing matched socks. My mother says I have felt this way for a long time. It has never posed a problem until now. Justin, 3—1\2 years old, also feels life is too short to worry about wearing matched socks. Deep down I think this is great, a chip off the old block; although, it could be hereditary because his Dad doesn't match them either, it's just not a statement with a drawer full of dark blue and black socks. But, now I hear myself reminding Justin to wear matched socks because we're going to the doctor's, to church, or shopping. To be fair I make every attempt to grab two of the same color. Why the slight concern? I'm investigating. Is it that I think he is too young to have a fashion statement? Do I feel I should be setting a better example so he can make the decision on the sock thing when he's older? Am I worried he'll tell someone "But my MOM doesn't wear socks that are the same!"

Oh well, I guess the damage is done. And besides, I'd have to change to expect something different and I'm too old for that. Life's too short.

Today started going bad three minutes after my eyes opened. My son needed discipline ten minutes after he rolled out of bed for a third offense. How does he do that? Everything possible that could fall or spill on the kitchen floor—was on the kitchen floor. It was foggy and still raining, with no relief in sight. When my husband came home in the morning from work we argued in front of the kids. Arguments, I feel, are okay in front of the kids if they understand the feelings are temporary and if they witness the settling or compromise. Husband went up for a nap in order to attend an afternoon meeting; there was no settling of differences. When we're strongly disagreeing on something, life is much harder. He's too much a major part of my life to have disrupted and expect things to go smoothly.

There was a small miracle—both children napped at the same time, so I did too—a very rare situation. A promise was made to usually napless son of reading twenty (he says twenty one) books before bed. His sister was on schedule to go to bed first, so we were really looking forward to the marathon reading time.

Another good hour came when together we flipped through old magazines for pictures to replace those on the kitchen cupboards for Rachel to smile at when she's cruising in her walker. She enjoys the baby faces on her level.

Then later, when I stepped out of the room for a minute, Rachel cried. Justin hurt her, which is something I don't handle well, even when I tell myself it's a normal sibling reaction on occasion. He explains what he's done and is sent to his room so I can cool off. He's usually so caring. Did I handle it right? The yelling is something I always feel guilty about, but it's hard not to be angry and disappointed with him for awhile.

The day just seemed to be filled with endless "no's," " don'ts," and "stop's." And there was also an exceedingly exasperating amount of "look, Mom," "watch me," or "can I's." Some days they're so easy to handle, today was not one of those days. My patience was elsewhere.

Husband came home from his meeting. We discussed areas of disagreement more. The situation improved, but was not mushy, yet. (Mushy is my favorite, but certainly not always possible). He retired in order to be ready for work in a few hours.

Evening arrived. Once both kids were bathed and fed, the time came for Rachel's rocking to sleep. If Justin makes too much noise, she'll refuse to close her eyes. He forgot this . . . her bottle emptied with her still awake. Maybe she'll sleep if I just lay her in her crib, I thought. No luck. She cried and disturbed husband. Back downstairs she screamed when I attempted to make her happy in her playpen. I glanced in frustrated frenzy at the mess that had taken over every room in the house. By this time I was wondering if it would be irresponsible of me to run away for a few hours. Would it take me out of contention for the Mother of the Year award?

Finally, I sat her on one side of me and him on the other for books. We did read six stories, but all I could think of was he still needed his teeth brushed, his fluoride pill, to go potty. Finally, he was ready for bed. She was at least playing quietly on the floor. He and I climbed the stairs for the tuck in. She screamed upon our departure. He got up after I tucked him in. Prayers were skipped to quicken my time to her before she woke her father. I urged him to do them alone. Quick tuck-ins I dislike; somehow relaxed moments prior to their eyes closing for the day seem important, but again, not always possible.

Downstairs I rocked her for twenty minutes before she finally fell asleep. It would have happened sooner if I had sung a sleepytime song, but I was in no mood for singing. His yawn was heard through the monitor so I tucked her in so he and I could talk one more time. As I knelt by his bed in an attempt to salvage the day in our last moments together until morning, he put his hands together asking for prayers. My insides relaxed a bit. We prayed for less arguing tomorrow, to be gentler with each other, for a happier day. We agreed getting along is more fun. He had just made up for every difficult moment he'd presented in the past thirteen hours. My insides stopped churning and I felt my body sighing the day's frustrations away.

The dishes still had to be done. The water they were in was cold from an earlier attempt, but it didn't bother me. The little prayer my son and I shared made me know tomorrow will be a better day. And I feel glad I'm a mom, again. But not every day is so easy, not every day is so easy.

More than ever I enjoy hearing an athlete, student, or whoever, being interviewed or spotted by a TV camera, wave and say "Hi, Mom!" My husband likes to believe he hears a greeting to both parents, but I know better. They know who gave birth to them.

Walks with my kids down "the lane" is one of our favorite ways to spend an afternoon. The path starts behind the barn and travels between fields, eventually coming by a woods if we walk far enough. It's an activity where no frustration arises because there's no need to say "no." We're carefree as we explore the nature around us. The hours are invaluable from a teaching aspect, for Justin remembers everything I mention concerning his surroundings. He's learned names of flowers, trees, birds, clouds, and animal tracks. Often he pushes his wheelbarrow or pulls his wagon to hold collectibles. Rachel always kicks excitedly in her stroller in anticipation of the adventure.

The soil in the beginning of the lane is very fine from heavy farm vehicle use. It is necessary to let it sift through our fingers and to make designs in it before putting a handful in the wheelbarrow or wagon. The last trip we made, as fall approached, was exciting because we found small wild grapes and chestnuts to add to the usual collection of stones, sticks, left over bean seeds from the field, Queen Ann's Lace, and wild asters. The prizes are carefully placed and constantly rearranged in the selected transporter.

Also on our most recent trip, we discovered an opening in the woods where a very large rock beckoned Justin to perch. It was there we found the chestnuts. Rachel was pushed in as far as the stroller would allow. The opening was called the "Secret Place;" we plan to take Daddy there as soon as possible.

Since Justin's been aware of keeping the earth clean he's been concerned with any garbage found, carelessly left by the ones working the fields or hunting. At first he would throw it off the path into the weeds, but now we store it in the basket under the stroller to put in the garbage can at home. It's hard for him to understand why we can't touch the large plastic containers found, even when I try to explain what could have been in them. These environmental lessons should pay off for a lifetime.

The walk back begins after a brief rest to snack on crackers or other goodies. We also take a moment to admire all the wheelbarrow or wagon is holding. A few grapes are squished to see how long the ink will stay on our fingers. Rachel is given something edible to hold. Our hike home is slow, but steady. Once in a while I find myself pushing the stroller and pulling a full wagon, but not often.

Back at home we settle under the pine trees or at the picnic table to put much of the collected in pails of water; Justin likes to soak things. Our cheeks hold a rosy glow; our appetites are hearty. After warm baths, I have two kids who fall asleep very soundly.

Ahhh . . . a walk down the lane, there's nothing like it.

A magical moment happened tonight. At 9:30 pm Justin woke with a bad dream of some sort; he never can remember the events to explain them to me. The night visions left him quite perplexed. Recognizing it as a true case of the creeps I carried him downstairs for a sip of milk hoping to distract him from the scary thoughts. He seemed relaxed so was returned to bed, but it was too soon for his aggravated state of mind returned. Sensing a need for merry chatter and bright lights (it always works for me) I carried him down again. We rocked while I chatted on about swing sets and slides, his favorite color red, and working outside with Grandpa. He was trying to dissolve whatever was bothering him. Then I noticed he was eyeing my music box on a very top shelf. At his request I let him wind it up, but it was broken from his prior investigating. I suggested we try my small jewelry music box; if it was a music box he needed, a music box he would get. We wound it up in the bathroom to hear the delightful *Music Box Dancer* melody. I picked him up and we danced lightly to the tune until it slowed and stopped. I caught his quick smile in the mirror. The small box was emptied of forgotten jewelry and taken into the living room. He wound it up and asked me to dance. Thus, the magical moment. My son and I danced to this merry tune in the quiet evening hours while the rest of the family was sleeping. We wound the key and swayed through the song three more times. It really was special.

After reading a few library books he was ready to be tucked in. I offered him the music box to take to bed, but

he declined. He did want it left on the coffee table though, for the morning. And you can bet it will be there.

Sometimes when I leave my husband with the kids for a few hours and I sense things are not going to go smoothly, I attempt to explain some "tricks of the trade" so to speak. I really should discuss these with him at a less hectic moment, instead of shouting the details on my way to the car.

For example, when our boy is in a mood to "help" with everything I need to do, I can relieve myself of this by having him wash his toy dishes in the sink. This water play keeps him near me, but out from under foot. Making a "pond" in the bathroom sink for ducks and Fisher Price people works great, too.

If one has time to set everything up, Justin will spend a good 45 minutes mixing ingredients for a snack. It only takes a minute or two to put granola cereal, raisins, oatmeal, peanut butter, and whatever else you can think of and depending on what time of day it is (I have been known to include mini marshmallows or chocolate chips) into separate little dishes. My little cook becomes totally absorbed in mixing the concoction and putting whatever doesn't make it in his belly, into mini muffin tins or as drop cookies on wax paper. Usually, Daddy is given one of the treats in his lunchbox, and the rest finds a place in the fridge, hopefully to be munched on at a later time. Unfortunately, the dough is much more fun to make than eat.

Our munchkin can also be kept content writing stories or grocery lists on any paper he has never seen before. I can usually dig up some blank recipe cards or note paper I'm never going to use for him to be quite excited about. This idea is only valuable if I am doing a project at the kitchen table, and feel I am able to keep up with his constant chatter.

In a desperate moment for peace he can be reminded of how much fun it is to make designs with dog biscuits or sort through and thread a tin of buttons.

Getting our three year old to "go potty" before going for a ride or before bed is a challenge I never anticipated experiencing. After a variety of attempts to complete the task with as little frustration as possible, I have discovered a routine that works almost every time: I excitedly tell the stubborn one to announce "zip-ah-de-do-dah day" when he has completed the chore. If he hints of giving trouble at this last routine before bed, I save the announcement of the "surprise secret word" until after the "water music" is over. He knows the word will get him a piggy-back ride to bed. Once I told him, with as much enthusiasm as I could muster, when I heard the "water music" I would sing "Raindrops Keep Falling On My Head". He knows all the words to that song now. It's surprising how creative one can get when confronted with a sticky situation, and interesting what song titles come to mind for the occasion. How do you explain these procedures to someone else?

Rachel can be kept busy for a few minutes, but not much more, by letting her eat Cheerios off of her high chair foot rest while she stands hanging on, although this back-fires when she's more entertained by hearing them scatter on the kitchen floor. In a desperate situation, such as when I have to put Justin to bed and she's in the mood to complain loudly about my few moments of absence, she can be quieted for a surprisingly long time with my car keys. This is important for a sleeping husband who works nights and has children who don't respond to "shhhhh" or come with volume controls.

Well anyway, they work for me. But when in a jam and desperate for a moment's peace, I'm sure my husband comes up with a few tricks of his own if he doesn't hear or remember the details I relay on my way out the door.

In the past few days it has come to my attention that every child who is close to the age of three and one half years, is presenting challenging behaviors, is displaying wild actions, is driving his parents crazy. It is also obvious that each mother is generally relieved when she discovers it's not just her child. One mom even found in text that challenging behavior, such as we had all witnessed, was common in the age of our children. We all appreciated the news and it quickly passed from one mom to the next. The information has given us the means to dig down a little deeper for saintly patience. Why, it's not us and our failing parenting skills, it's them! Oh, happy day!!

It just goes to show—we should always keep talking. Friends have invaluable information. And we mothers need all the understanding friends, and information, we can get.

Today I received a letter from a friend. She mentioned how her children were doing, as most mothers do. She happened to mention her two year old was displaying temper tantrums. Now why did this bit of information make me smile so? It seems I thoroughly enjoy it when someone's kid is driving them crazy. Someone suggested "misery loves company" and I think that about explains it. It's not that I wish difficult days for my friends, but I love to hear the details when one lands in their week. Somehow the sharing of such moments is going to bring us all the closer and it will defiantly assist in keeping one's perspective.

The introduction of a newborn results in a state of total exhaustion which leads to a state of indecisiveness. I recall spending several, or more, minutes with these 2:00 a.m. thoughts: Shall I change her diaper? Maybe she's not too wet. But, she has had a lot to drink. But that would really wake her up. I wonder, if she did wake up, how long would it take to get her back to sleep. She could lay in bed with me.

No, then I will have dreams of rolling on her for weeks. I'll just put her back in her crib. But she'll be so uncomfortable if she wets through. Well, let's skip the change. Now, I wonder if I should lay her on her back or tummy. If she is on her back, she could choke on spits. If she is on her tummy, she could lay in spits. Maybe I should just hold her here, in my arms, rocking, until morning. It is her favorite place you know, and she's perfectly comfortable here. Sleep tight, Pumpkin.

I must confess, I have never actually come to this decision; it just seemed to be a peaceful ending to the problem at the time of writing. Now that my Pumpkin is ten months old, and still waking in the night, my 2:00 am thoughts are quite different: "If she doesn't stop crying in one more minute I'm going to give her a bottle and hope she sleeps until at least 5:30 am." I stumble to her crib, position nipple in lips, and stumble back to bed hoping sleep will overtake me as soon as possible.

My girl's temperature finally broke. It lasted three nights and two days, the result of a DPT vaccine and a terrible cold. She's been miserable, she hasn't slept, she's needed her mommy. During this time life stood still. The dishes piled up. The hamper overflowed. Meals served did not require cooking. I rocked, and rocked, and rocked. I took her temperature, administered medicine, and tried to make her comfortable. Her few moments of contentment, or sleep, were spent in giving attention to her brother.

When my kids are sick I pray more. Little prayers throughout the day and night, asking (pleading) for a healing hand to make them better, to restore health to my baby. When the fever breaks and other symptoms of concern fade and it's evident all is well, when my child's eyes smile and dance, I experience a moment of pure happiness and relief. I thank God. It happens everytime.

More than once I have pondered over what my thoughts for God would be if my child did not regain his health. How would my love and faith in Him change? Maybe my immediate response would be anger and denial of His existence. I would probably vow never to pray or attend church again. However, these feelings would be directed toward the heavens; I know He would be listening and I would loudly, tearfully, and constantly let Him know what I thought of His plan. In my sorrow I would a thousand times ask Him "why." But the questions would be directed to Him; how else would I ever survive a tragedy such as this? I pray I never have to find out.

At the school where I was teaching there is (was?) a questionnaire type form for parents of in-coming kinder-gartners to fill out. The answers help the child's teacher know their students better. There is one request on the form that has never left my thoughts for very long since the day I read it. The request was to describe your child . . . in one sentence. Now, I can certainly understand the need for parents to keep the description brief, and I myself benefited from the sentences from the role of teacher; however, I have yet to even begin to consider how I as a parent would complete this task.

Should I simply list my son's characteristics? But, shouldn't the teacher be aware of what situations bring out his even more active self? And his personality certainly changes when he's tired or hungry. Just how many commas and semi-colons are we allowed in this sentence? I don't recall how much space was allowed for the description. Did they suggest using the back of the paper if one needed more room?

As a teacher I now wonder why I didn't see more sentences simply stating, "My son/daughter is the most wonderful little person you could ever hope to have for a student; he/she is extremely intelligent, beautiful, friendly, loving, and helpful; please take the best care of him/her."

After all this thought I realize, to even greater depths, how vital our teacher's love of children, dedication to education, and effectiveness are to the children, our children, absorbing everything in their classrooms. There is no doubt in my mind that becoming a mother has greatly enhanced my role as a teacher.

Sigh . . . I still have a few years to work on that sentence. Maybe it's not on the form anymore.

Sometimes I think about how life would be different if for some reason my husband and I had decided not to have children. (I don't include here the possibility of wanting, but unable to conceive, for that is a wholly different set of circumstances.)

We would have more time alone together . . . but, would we cherish it so much? We would be able to go out to dinner more often . . . but, peanut butter and jelly and McDonald's drive thru aren't all that bad. The house would be more sophisticated looking, rather than resembling a pre-school . . . but, it will have plants, walls without projects displayed, and more room to walk someday. We would have a newer car and two vehicles in the driveway . . . but, we really never need two now. I would be teaching . . . but, the schools will still be there when I'm ready. We'd be rich . . . but, except for more books and more dinners out, there's nothing I can think of that we need or want. I would have more time to work on this book . . . but, there would be no thoughts on being a mommy to write about.

Our children . . . our treasures, it seems I'm rich after all.

The conclusion of this collection of thoughts, but the writing continues . . . because the mothering continues.

Mother–Love––Child–Love

My child
precious one
I'd give you
the moon, the stars, the sun.
I'll give you hugs and kisses
until each day is done.

I'll teach you
all I understand of life.
I'll welcome you warmly
in the morning light
and gently tuck you in at night.

I'll pray you have a
life of smiles.
I'll always have time
to talk for awhile.
I'll tell you often
how I love my child.

But you'll never, never understand
how strong is my love for you
until one day
you'll hold your babe
and then feel mother-love-child-love, too.

by Karla Borglum Santoro

Child's Plea

Talk to me the child pleads,
Smile, I'll know you care.
Talk to me the child pleads,
Touch me, I'll know you're there.
I need your love, love, love.

Don't lead me astray, take me through your day.
Share your thoughts about the sun.
Today I can't speak, but my smile will grow
For how I love to listen.
I need your love, love, love.

Please take some time to read to me.
Teach me right from wrong.
All my trust I give to you,
Teach me the rhythm to life's song.
I need your love, love, love.

Show me life, the simple things.
Keep me safe, oh share a smile.
Show me please the Lord is my God,
Talk about Him for awhile.
Please just a little while.
I need His love, love, love.

Love your husband, love your wife
For your child a part of you.
From you this being learns of life,
Give him the best of you.
They need your love, love, love.
All your love, love, love.
Just your love, love, love.

by Karla Borglum Santoro

The author with her husband, Mark,
and children, Justin and Rachel.

About the author . . .

Karla Borglum Santoro taught kindergarten before combining full-time mothering with a variety of very part-time jobs, including photographing children, conducting summer story hours, and helping adults gain their high school diplomas. She eagerly anticipates returning to the elementary school classroom because teaching children is her passion. In the meantime, the author writes for children, and about children. This is her first book about children . . . more specifically, about being their mother. Mrs. Santoro lives with her husband, Mark, and their children, Justin and Rachel, in upstate New York.